HABITATS

COASTS

DAVID CUMMING

RSVP

RAINTREE
STECK-VAUGHN
P U B L I S H E R S

The Steck-Vaughn Company

Austin, Texas

H A B I T A T S

Coasts	**Mountains**
Deserts	**Polar Regions**
Forests	**Rivers and Lakes**
Grasslands	**Oceans and Seas**
Islands	**Wetlands**

Cover: "The Twelve Apostles" off the coast of Victoria, Australia

Title page: Crescent Beach in Oregon

Contents page: Tidepools at Seal Rock State Park in Oregon

Published by Raintree Steck-Vaughn Publishers, an imprint of Steck-Vaughn Company

Library of Congress Cataloging-in-Publication Data
Cumming, David.
Coasts / David Cumming.
    p.   cm.—(Habitats)
    Includes bibliographical references and index.
    Summary: Describes coastal erosion, deposition, wildlife, and pollution.
    ISBN 0-8172-4520-0
    1. Coasts—Juvenile literature.
    2. Coastal ecology—Juvenile literature.
    [1. Coasts. 2. Coastal ecology. 3. Ecology.]
    I. Title. II. Series: Habitats (Austin, Tex.)
    GB451.2.C86   1997
    574.5'2638—dc20   96-8364

Printed in Italy. Bound in the United States.
1 2 3 4 5 6 7 8 9 0 01 00 99 98 97

CONTENTS

1. WHERE THE SEA MEETS THE LAND

The coast is the place where the sea meets the land. So the coastline of a country is all its land that borders the sea.

When people say they are off to the coast, they usually mean they are going to the beach or to the seashore. Properly speaking though, the coast consists of more than the seashore itself: It also includes the narrow strip of land that extends from a little inland to a little offshore. It is a habitat with three important variations. The inland coastal habitat is always in the open air. The beach, however, is covered by the sea half the time. And the land offshore is underwater all the time.

There are various kinds of coasts. In some, the land slopes gently into the sea. In others it ends abruptly at steep, high cliffs. The type of land in coastal regions also varies, from soggy swamps or fine, golden sand to boulders and tall, jagged rocks. In very cold places, such as Antarctica, the coastline is buried all year beneath a thick layer of ice and snow.

The golden sands of Palm Cove Beach, on the Queensland coast of northeast Australia

High, steep cliffs drop into the Atlantic Ocean on the west coast of Ireland.

Like all land, the coast is under constant attack from the weather. Unprotected by hills or mountains, it is exposed to the full destructive force of the wind and rain, snow and ice. In addition, the coast has to contend with the sea. And the sea plays a double role, for it destroys the coast as well as creating more of it. However, it is as a destroyer that the sea makes its biggest impact on the coast. In order to survive, coastal plants and animals have developed unique ways of dealing with the constant battering of waves and wind. Likewise, the coast's human inhabitants have struggled for centuries to protect themselves from the invading sea.

The mountainous coast of Antarctica, which is buried all year beneath thick ice and snow

5

2. COASTAL EROSION

The coast comes under heaviest attack from nature during a storm, when it can be lashed simultaneously by strong winds, heavy rain, and mighty waves. In the process the coast is worn away, or eroded. Although the weather plays a part in the coast's erosion, the waves cause the most damage.

The power of waves

Waves are made by the wind blowing over the sea and forming ripples, which gradually grow bigger and bigger. The stronger the wind, the higher and more powerful the waves will be. Tall, powerful waves are also made by the wind if it has blown a long way over the sea.

Out at sea, waves appear to be water on the move, but this is an illusion. Where the sea is deep, it is the shape of the wave that moves through the sea, not the seawater itself. Think of holding a rope and flicking it: The rope remains in your hand, but a "wave" travels along it. Waves at sea behave in just the same way.

The behavior of waves changes when they arrive in the shallow water along the coast. The shallows slow the waves, making their tops, or crests, curl over and "break" into a frothy foam called surf. Now, not only the shape of the wave is moving, but the water itself. That is why surfers can be pushed along by breaking waves.

A surfer makes use of the awesome power of a breaking wave.

A breaking wave has enormous power, and the bigger the wave, the greater its power to erode. Breaking storm waves can pound against the coast with a force of approximately 70 tons per square yard.

How waves erode the coast

Over hundreds of thousands of years, the coastline changes. When waves crash onto the coast during storms, they compress the air trapped in the land's cracks and joints. As the waves fall back, the sudden release of pressure acts like an explosion, widening the cracks and joints. This "hydraulic action" weakens the land, and chunks of it eventually fall into the sea. The sea then uses this material to erode the coast even more.

Waves like these thunder against the coast and erode it.

Terrible damage caused by a tidal wave that swept away a coastal railroad in southern India in 1964

Tsunamis—waves of destruction

Ocean waves are caused by winds, but a tsunami, or tidal wave, is different: It is created by an earthquake in the seabed. Vibrations from the earthquake cause the sea above to fan out in ripples, which travel at speeds of up to 500 mph. Despite their speed, these waves are not harmful because they are low. However, the shallows off a coast act like a brake, and the waves rear up into giants, as much as 200 feet tall. These crash down on coastal land with terrible consequences. Whole villages can be wiped out in seconds. Little can be done to prevent this destruction, but sometimes there is enough time to warn people to flee inland.

Broken boulders and lumps of rock from the land are thrown against the coast in storms, causing further damage. Wearing away the land in this way is called abrasion.

During the abrasion process, boulders and rocks collide and break into smaller stones. As they crash and grind together in the waves on the shore, the stones' rough edges are knocked off and they become smooth, rounded pebbles. This process is known as attrition. Next, the pebbles are ground to shingle. Finally, the waves grind the pebbles into grains of sand.

Seawater itself is slightly acidic, so it can destroy coastal land by dissolving it. This is called corrosion. Soft rocks, such as chalk and limestone, dissolve more quickly than do hard ones, like granite, so coasts made with soft rocks will disappear sooner than those containing hard rocks.

Pools of seawater are often left in hollows in the rocks when the tide goes out. Crabs and shrimps, for example, get trapped in these tide pools and must wait for high tide to escape.

Erosion by the weather

The weather also plays a part in eroding the coast. Like seawater, rain is acidic, so it eats away the land. It trickles into cracks in soft rocks, dissolving and weakening them. In colder climates, during the winter, the rain freezes at night in the cracks in hard rocks. During the day, the sun melts the ice. This freezing-and-thawing action shatters the rocks. Strong winds, too, can blow away loose pieces in the top layer of coastal land. Any sand and grit carried by these winds acts like sandpaper, rubbing away at the land.

Limestone is a soft rock that is easily worn away by the weather and the sea. These cliffs show how the limestone has been eaten away.

The results of erosion

Where there is high land along a coast, waves eat into its base to form a notch. The notch becomes deeper and deeper until the land overhanging it collapses, leaving a steep-faced cliff. The sea will make a notch in the cliff's base, and its face will eventually tumble down. As the erosion continues, the cliff is left with a flat rocky beach in front of it, called a wave-cut platform, where the cliff once stood.

Many coastlines are made of areas of soft and hard rock. The soft rock is eroded first into bays, leaving the hard rock jutting out to sea as headlands.

This diagram shows how the coast is eroded to form cliffs and wave-cut platforms.

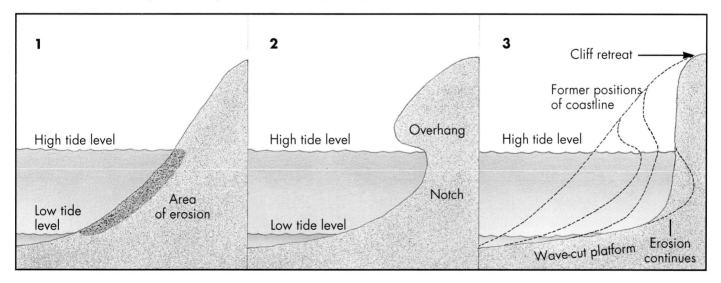

1

High tide level

Low tide level

Area of erosion

2

High tide level

Low tide level

Overhang

Notch

3

Cliff retreat

Former positions of coastline

High tide level

Wave-cut platform

Erosion continues

Pebbles cover much of this wave-cut platform. The cliffs are made of chalk, a soft rock, which erodes quickly.

Because it juts out, a headland is not sheltered, so any holes or cracks in it will soon be made bigger by the waves. Sometimes, a hole in a headland's base is enlarged and becomes a cave. Air trapped in the cave will be squeezed upward, forcing it into cracks in the roof. In time, this hydraulic action

Seawater sprays out of a blowhole —a crack in the rock formed as air is squeezed upward by the power of waves.

The sea has created several natural arches through this ancient headland on the coast of Bermuda.

will create a blowhole in the top of the headland through which the air can escape.

Sometimes, the back walls of caves on either side of a headland are worn away so that they meet in the middle, creating an arch. If the arch falls, the tip of the headland becomes a tiny island, called a stack.

These diagrams show the features found in headlands because of the sea's action.

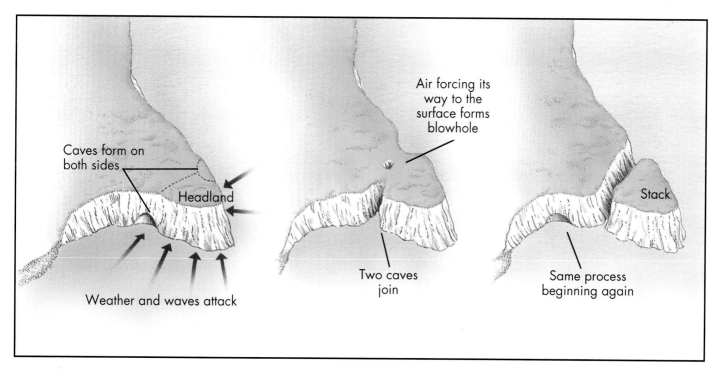

Caves form on both sides

Headland

Weather and waves attack

Air forcing its way to the surface forms blowhole

Two caves join

Stack

Same process beginning again

3. COASTAL DEPOSITION

Much of what the sea erodes from one part of the coast is deposited farther along it, extending the shore. This coastal deposition happens because of a process called longshore drift.

Longshore drift

A wave is known as swash when it hits the shore after breaking. The water that drains back into the sea is called backwash.

Waves travel in straight lines out at sea. However, they are bent when they enter shallow water, so they break at an angle to the shore. Consequently, the swash goes up the shore at an angle. The backwash, however, travels

This aerial photograph shows breakwaters along the shore. They stop longshore drift, so pebbles carried by the sea are dropped and build up next to the breakwaters.

This diagram illustrates the process of longshore drift.

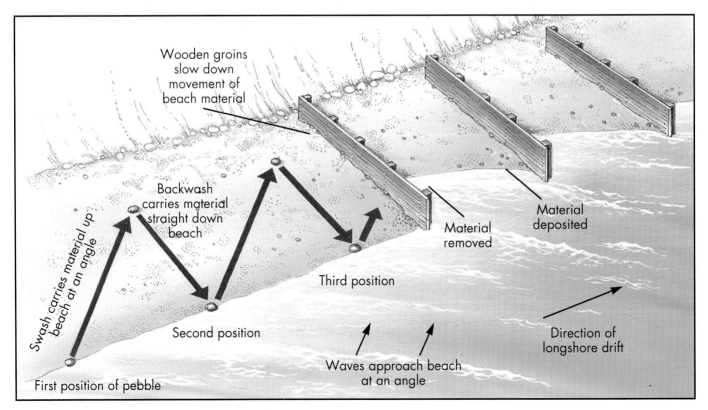

Wooden groins slow down movement of beach material

Backwash carries material straight down beach

Swash carries material up beach at an angle

Second position

First position of pebble

Third position

Material removed

Material deposited

Waves approach beach at an angle

Direction of longshore drift

straight down to the sea. Thus a pebble carried up by the swash and brought down by the backwash will end up farther along the shore from where it started. After this has happened repeatedly, the pebble will be far from its starting point. This is how longshore drift moves shore material along the coast.

The direction of the longshore drift varies, depending on which direction the wind is blowing from. Winds generally blow from one direction, so on a particular stretch of coast, material is moved consistently in one direction.

Beaches

Longshore drift transports sand and pebbles along the coast until something blocks its way and causes it to drop its load. The obstruction is often a headland, in which case the load will become a beach in the bay sheltered by the headland. Beaches can be muddy as well as sandy or stony.

A variety of rock colors can be seen in the cliffs of Alum Bay on the Isle of Wight, off the south coast of England.

Beaches of different colors
Since sand is ground-up rock, its color comes from the rock's color. Golden sand, for example, comes from rocks rich in quartz, a yellow mineral. Beaches can also have brown or black sand. Some sand is formed from ground-up seashells or coral (see page 29), so it can be white or pink.

This is the Mississippi River Delta in the Gulf of Mexico. The delta's land is made from layers and layers of silt dropped over the centuries by the river when it enters the sea.

Deltas

At the start of its journey to the sea, river water is clear. By the end of its journey, silt will have made it murky. Silt is a muddy mixture of soil, rocks, and stones eroded from the land and ground into fine particles by the river as it flows along. The river deposits the silt at its mouth, or estuary. The silt gradually builds up into mud banks, or mudflats, in and alongside the estuary.

The Ganges and Brahmaputra rivers of India enter the Indian Ocean through one mouth at the top of the Bay of Bengal. Together, these two giant Asian rivers carry nearly 1 billion tons of silt. This is more than double the amount of silt transported to the ocean by the Mississippi River and all its tributaries.

A large river brings down so much silt that its estuary becomes blocked with muddy islands. This "new" land creeps out into the ocean, forming a delta. Instead of entering the sea through one mouth, the river crisscrosses the delta land and exits through many channels. Huge deltas have been formed by rivers such as the Ganges, Nile, Mississippi, and Volga. Their muddy beaches extend for many miles along the coast.

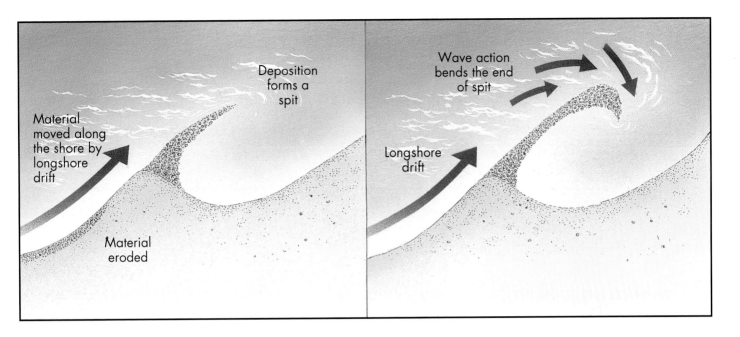

Spits, bars, and tombolos

Like headlands, estuaries and bays disrupt longshore drift and force it to drop its load. In an estuary, the deposited material can extend, like a huge, curved finger, into the river's mouth. This is called a spit.

In a bay, on the other hand, the deposited material can develop into a bar. Unlike a spit, this extends across the bay, cutting it off from the sea. The lake that forms behind the bar is called a lagoon. Its water is salty because waves can pour over the bar.

A tombolo is also made up of deposited material and is similar to a bar, but it stretches between the shore and a nearby island. It joins the island to the mainland.

The formation of a spit by the action of longshore drift

This sandy tombolo joins an island in the Indian Ocean to the mainland of Iran.

4. TIDES AND CURRENTS

Coastal erosion and deposition are influenced by the tides and offshore currents.

Tides

In most areas of the world the sea rises and falls twice a day. Tides cause these daily changes in sea level. At high tide the water level is at its highest; at low tide it is lowest.

The pull of the moon and sun's gravity is the main reason for tides. The moon's pull is twice as powerful as the sun's because it is much nearer the earth. Tides are also affected by the spin of the earth, as well as by the shape of the seabed and the coastline. However, it is the positions of the sun and moon in relation to the earth that are most important.

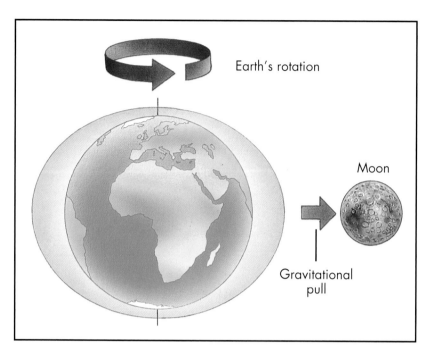

Earth's rotation

Moon

Gravitational pull

Above The spin of the earth and gravity cause the oceans to bulge and the tides to rise and fall.

Left An exceptionally high spring tide flooded this fairground in Norfolk, on the east coast of England.

On the side of the earth facing the moon, the oceans are pulled outward in a bulge. Meanwhile, on the opposite side, the spinning of the earth creates another bulge. These bulges produce the high tides. The low tides are the troughs between them.

Twice a month, the sun and moon are in line—that is, pulling on the earth together. These are the spring tides, when the high tides are extra high and the low tides are extra low. At spring high tides, the sea reaches its highest point on the shore. At spring low tides, the sea drops to its lowest point, and the difference between high and low tide is very great. At low spring tide, the whole beach will be uncovered.

Each month there are also two neap tides, when the sun, earth, and moon form a right angle. On these occasions, the sun reduces the pull of the moon's gravity. The difference between high and low neap tides is very small. The high tides do not reach far up the shore, and the low tides do not go far down it. So at low neap tide only a little of the beach is uncovered.

These diagrams show the tidal cycle every month of spring and neap tides.

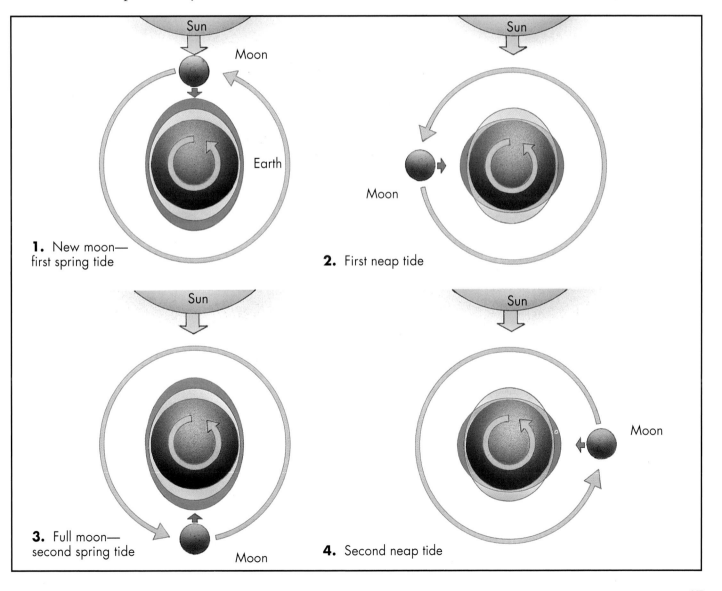

1. New moon—first spring tide

2. First neap tide

3. Full moon—second spring tide

4. Second neap tide

Tides allow the sea to erode a greater area of the coast than if the sea level never changed. Spring high tides allow waves to cause destruction higher up the shore. A cliff face can be battered by stones and boulders when a storm occurs at the same time as these high tides. Spring high tides will also deposit material higher up the shore.

Strand lines

After a high tide, the water goes back down the beach, leaving a strand line of debris washed up by the waves. Spring high tides will form a strand line high up the beach, below which will be a series of strand lines from lower tides. Strand lines contain all sorts of materials, from seaweed and shells to household trash and fishing equipment.

Trash along the high-tide strand line of a beach

Currents

The rise and fall of tides are an important cause of the currents off the coast. Unlike waves, currents are water on the move. Even so, they are not as strong as waves. Currents can be responsible for part of coastal deposition. While waves can carry stones, currents are only strong enough to transport sand and silt. Like longshore drift (*see pages 12–13*), when they are slowed by obstacles or gaps along the coast, currents will drop their load. Spits and bars build up as material is left on them by currents.

Currents can also be destructive and erode the coast. They are most harmful when forced by the tide through narrow gaps or up and down river estuaries. The water can then pick up enough speed to shift sandbanks and mudflats.

Currents have a great effect on the climate along a coast. The cold Humboldt Current, for example, flows up the west coast of South America. Winds blowing across the Humboldt Current are cooled, so when they reach the warm land, fogs form. The North Atlantic Drift is a warm current that flows around the western side of the British Isles to Norway. As a result, part of Scotland's coast is hot enough for palm trees to grow, and Norway's ports do not freeze in winter.

Although it is above the Arctic Circle, the Norwegian port of Hammerfest does not freeze in winter, thanks to the warm North Atlantic Drift.

5. CHANGES IN SEA LEVEL

Some 18,000 years ago the world was much colder than it is today. It was so cold, in fact, that most of northern Europe, Asia, and North America was buried beneath glaciers over a mile thick. During this period, known as the Ice Age, the oceans were at their lowest level ever: Three times more water was stored as ice in the glaciers than in the oceans. Then, around 10,000 years ago, temperatures rose and nearly all the glaciers melted.

The end of the Ice Age affected coasts in the following two ways.

Coastal submergence

Following the Ice Age, the melting ice drained into the sea, raising its level from the all-time low. The sea level increased by as much as 500 feet in some places. Inevitably, this meant that a lot of coastal land was submerged.

River valleys were flooded by the sea, forming the rias that can be seen along the coasts of New Zealand, northwestern Spain, and southwestern England.

The rise in sea level at the end of the Ice Age allowed the sea to eat its way farther inland along many coasts.

The Dalmatian coasts were created where river valleys were parallel to the coast—not at right angles, as in the case of rias. A good example can be seen on the coast of Croatia: The hilltops along the edge of the old coast protrude through the surface of the Adriatic Sea. Once part of the mainland, the hilltops are now islands.

During the Ice Age, glaciers gouged out the sides and bottoms of many valleys. Some of the glaciers even eroded the valley bottoms far below sea level. When the glaciers melted and the sea level rose, these valleys filled with water to become fiords, like the ones in Alaska, Norway, Chile, and New Zealand's South Island. Fiords are usually narrow, steep-sided and very deep. The Sogne Fiord in Norway, for example, is 13,379 feet deep, and the Messier Channel in Chile is 13,671 feet deep.

A barrier island off North Carolina continues to grow with sand dropped by longshore drift.

Barrier islands

Barrier islands are found off the coasts of many countries. They protect the coast from the worst seas, hence, their name. The most impressive are the string of narrow islands stretching for 2,976 miles down the eastern coast of the United States into the Gulf of Mexico. Most geographers think that global warming was responsible for their formation. When the sea rose at the end of the Ice Age, tall sand dunes on the coast became offshore islands.

A view of the Aurland Fiord on the coast of Norway

Coastal emergence

The thick glaciers formed during the last Ice Age were very heavy. Their weight pressed down on the land and made it sink. After the glaciers had melted, the land rose. Parts of the coast that were once beneath the sea were soon above it, having emerged from underwater. Northwestern Scotland, for example, is still rising by about 0.16 inches a year. In Scandinavia, the increase is about 0.8 inches a year. In these places, coastal land has risen many feet since the end of the Ice Age.

Once beside the sea, this harbor at Blakeney, England, is now joined to it by a channel.

Consequently, beaches and cliffs that were once by the side of the sea have been lifted above it. A raised beach is a beach that is now high and always dry. Towns, too, that once had harbors have sometimes ended up several miles from the sea.

It is possible that this Maldive island may be drowned by the Indian Ocean in the not-too-distant future.

Global warming and the coast

The build up of "greenhouse gases" in the atmosphere is preventing heat from escaping and is making the earth warmer. Scientists fear that if ice at the North and South poles melts, the sea level will rise and flood low coastal land. Indeed, whole islands could disappear. For example, if the sea level increased by just 10 feet, the Maldive Islands in the Indian Ocean would vanish beneath the waves.

The latest information reveals that the sea level has been increasing by 0.12 inches a year for the past two years—twice as fast as scientists thought.

6. COASTAL WILDLIFE

The coast is home to many types of plants and animals, the largest variety of which can be seen along the shore. Here, where land and sea overlap, a whole range of flora and fauna can be found, from those that are accustomed to living in the open air to those that are used to spending virtually all their lives underwater.

Zones on the seashore

The shore can be divided into four different zones. The splash, or spray zone runs along the top of the shore. This strip of land is just above the highest point reached by the tide. It becomes wet only when splashed by waves in stormy weather or at spring high tides. The upper zone lies below the spray zone. This is the part of the shore that is covered only by spring high tides. The middle zone is next, and is the widest of all the zones. It is covered and uncovered twice a day by the incoming and outgoing tides. Finally, there is the lower zone, which is nearly always underwater and only uncovered at the spring low tides. The particular plants and animals found in these zones will depend on the type of shore.

This diagram shows the different zones of the seashore.

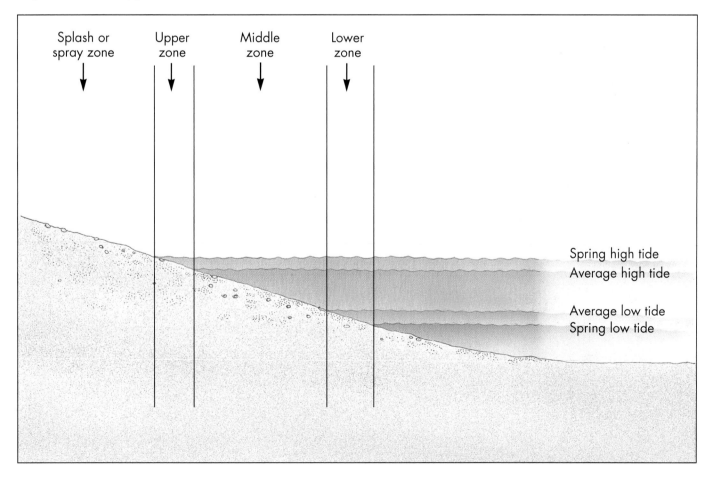

Splash or spray zone

Upper zone

Middle zone

Lower zone

Spring high tide
Average high tide

Average low tide
Spring low tide

Life in muddy estuaries

A river mouth has the widest range of plants and animals of all the places on the seashore. Its mudflats consist of silt, which is rich in the nutrients plants need in order to grow well. Many animals also find the silt very nourishing. Fresh silt arrives all the time, and twice a day the tide brings in a new supply of seawater, which is full of oxygen and the tiny bits of organic debris and plankton eaten by shore creatures. Not surprisingly, the plants and animals living in the estuaries thrive. In turn, they attract many birds and fishes that enjoy eating them.

The mudflats never dry out completely because droplets of water remain trapped inside the mud. Even the land in the splash zone is marshy. So plants that like soggy soils grow in estuaries. The smaller the plant, the higher up the mudflats it will be, to escape drowning by the tide. Some plants, though, adapt their growth to cope with the high water levels. The sea aster, for example, is usually short, but in estuaries it can grow three feet tall to allow its flowers to remain in the air at high tide.

When the tide goes out, there is more river water in the estuary than seawater. However, at high tide the water will be saltier because the sea has

Taller-than-usual sea asters growing in an estuary

Like most estuary creatures, crabs can survive both in river water and seawater.

Above Long roots prevent mangrove trees from being swept away by the tides.

Above This mudskipper is at home on land and in water.

Mangroves and mudskippers

There are mangrove forests on the muddy banks of many river estuaries on coasts near the equator. A mangrove tree has two types of roots. Long roots trail down from the branches into the mud to keep the tree upright in the waves at high tide. Another set of roots protrudes up through the mud to breathe in oxygen at low tide. They absorb oxygen from the air because there is little in the soggy mud.

Mudskippers live among the mangrove trees. They are small fish that are amphibious (able to live on land and in water). When the tide is in, they swim and breathe underwater. When the tide is out, the mudskippers can breathe in the open air while hopping around on the mud on their strong fins.

pushed the river water back upstream. Estuary animals have to cope with changes in the water's saltiness. Crabs, for example, can survive in estuaries because they are able to alter the amount of salt in their blood. Since they prefer salty water, the crabs increase the amount of salt in their blood when the water becomes less salty.

The long legs of this American avocet enable it to hunt for food in the shallow waters at low tide.

Shrimps, lugworms, and shellfish are often found in estuaries because there they can easily hide from predators in the soft mud. This is particularly the case at low tide when birds such as herons and curlews arrive to wade through the shallows on their long legs in search of a meal. These birds also have long bills to pry out lugworms and shrimps near the mud's surface.

Pebble beaches

Compared with all the wildlife activity in an estuary, a pebble beach is a very quiet place. To learn why few plants or animals live there, visit a pebble beach during a storm, but make sure you stay well away from the water's edge. You will hear—perhaps even be deafened by—the noise of millions of stones grinding against each other. Watch, too, as the stones are thrown onto nearby land and tumble about in the swash and backwash. Then imagine what it would be like to be a plant or animal on that beach: Even a tough shell would not protect you from serious damage.

The splash zone is the safest area. In the summer, birds such as terns, ringed plovers, and oystercatchers nest among the wild cabbages growing there.

Puffins shelter on a cliff on the Shetland Islands, north of the Scottish mainland.

Cliff creatures and plants

Life on a steep, windswept cliff face would seem to be impossible. True, it is not easy, especially during storms, but birds and plants can survive there. Birds such as ravens, peregrine falcons, gannets, guillemots, and cormorants build their nests on ledges on cliff faces. Storm petrels like more sheltered, well-hidden nests, so they make them in large cracks or inside sea-cliff caves. Plants also grow on ledges and in crevices where a layer of soil has been trapped. Their seeds may have been blown there by the wind or dropped by birds. Species like rock samphire, rock sea lavender, and rock sea campion thrive on the salty spray from the sea. On top of cliffs, away from the sea spray, grasses, small trees, and bushes grow in the thin, poor soils. Sheep and cattle can be seen grazing here, alongside rabbits digging their burrows.

Sandy shores

At first glance, sandy shores seem as empty as stony ones. But look closer. Notice the worm casts (the little mounds of sand thrown out by lugworms) and the outline of a half-buried starfish. Like an estuary's mudflats, the sand contains hundreds of hidden occupants: Along with the lugworms and starfish, there are shrimps, snails, sea urchins, and many, many others.

If they lived on top of the sand, life would be dangerous for these small creatures. At low tide they would be exposed to hungry birds, the hot sun, or freezing winds. At high tide, they would be at the mercy of powerful waves and hungry fish. So they are more secure beneath the sand's surface, where the temperature hardly changes and there are few enemies. At low tide, these "burrowers" dig themselves into the sand. At high tide, they return to the surface of the sand to feed.

The lugworm is a typical sand creature. It can measure up to 8 inches long, and lives in a U-shaped tunnel with two holes. The lugworm wriggles in and out of one hole and uses the other for waste disposal. At high tide it leaves its home to fill itself with sand. Returning underground, it digests any edible particles in the sand and rejects the rest, which form worm casts on the sand's surface.

The casts make it easy for fishermen to find lugworms. Fishermen dig them up to use as bait on their hooks, because fish find it difficult to resist a fat, juicy lugworm.

28

The world's largest coral reef
The Great Barrier Reef stretches for 1,240 miles along the coast of northeastern Australia—and it is alive! The reef has been formed by polyps, tiny creatures with a hard skeleton. They are related to sea anemones. About 20 million years ago, the ancestors of the present polyps started the reef. When they died, their skeletons sank to the seabed and new polyps began to grow on top of them. A coral reef slowly formed growing higher and wider and longer year by year—and it is still growing.

An aerial photograph of Hardy Lagoon, part of the Great Barrier Reef, off the coast of Queensland, Australia

Often, the wind blows sand inland, piling it into dunes in the spray zone behind the beach. The dunes can reach the height of small hills on some coasts. On the sea-facing slopes of dunes, only certain grasses, such as sand couch, lyme, and marram, can withstand the salty spray. They have rhizomes—unusual rootlike stems— from which both long roots and shoots grow very quickly. The roots easily stretch down into the soil underneath the sand to absorb moisture and nutrients. New shoots soon sprout from stems that are smothered by any sand building on top of them. Hunting and jumping spiders live on the stems, spinning webs to entangle passing flies and gnats. Black-headed gulls and red-winged blackbirds build their nests among the grass tussocks. The inland slopes of the dunes are covered with clumps of scrub, which are home to rabbits.

Marram grass growing in sand dunes behind a beach

Rocky shores

If burrowers survive best on sandy shores, "hangers-on" are better suited to rocky shores. Most of these hangers-on are crustaceans, mollusks, and snails, whose soft bodies are protected by hard shells. They live in the middle and lower coastal zones, feeding off the plankton brought in at high tide.

Each of these little creatures possesses a muscle that protrudes from the shell and allows them to stick firmly to the rock, even in the most stormy weather.

This whelk uses its single "foot" to clamp itself to rocks so that it is not washed away by waves.

No matter how firmly a mollusk adheres to a rock, an oystercatcher's thin, pointed beak can reach down between a rock and a shell and lever it off. The oystercatcher likes all mollusks, including mussels. It tries to find mussels that are feeding, because then their shells will be open and it can spear the flesh inside with its beak. Should the mussel snap shut on its hunter's beak, the oystercatcher has the strength to force its shells apart. Seagulls also eat mollusks. They pick them up and then

An oystercatcher guards its eggs. Its beak is strong enough to pry apart the shells of mussels and other shellfish.

drop them from a height onto a rock or road to shatter the shell. High tide brings other enemies: Lobsters and large crabs can smash the shells with their claws.

The most common plant on the shore, seaweed, also has to hang on for survival. To do this it has developed rootlike "holdfasts" that grip the rocks tightly. Seaweed has two other characteristics to enable it to spend its life in the open air or underwater. To prevent its drying out at low tide, seaweed has a sticky covering over its fronds (leaves). Seaweed is also very flexible, so it bends and sways in the waves and currents. If it were rigid, the swirling waters would tear it.

These female California sea lions have settled on a rocky beach to give birth to their pups.

Different varieties of seaweed on a beach in western France

Seaweed: A plant with many uses

• *It provides food and shelter for coastal creatures.*

• *Although it does not appeal to everyone, seaweed is full of vitamins, and is a nutritious food. In China and Japan, large quantities are eaten; in Wales it is used to make a special type of bread.*

• *Farmers living near coasts spread seaweed on their fields as a fertilizer; in Iceland and northern France, they feed it to pigs and horses.*

• *Seaweed is used to make glue, soap, medicines, and all sorts of food, from ice cream and salad dressing to edible sausage skin.*

7. PEOPLE ON THE COAST

Throughout history, a country's coast has been a natural resource that humans have put to good use.

Seafood

The first settlers on the coast were attracted by the abundant supply of fish in the sea. Soon the fish became more than just food: Villages were built where the people earned a living from fish—catching and then selling their catch inland. As farming developed, many nations turned to eating meat, and fishing declined.

Modern technology has meant that fishing has become easier. This has led to overfishing—a dangerous reduction in the numbers of fish—which has also contributed to the closing of fishing ports. However, in many poor countries, fish is cheaper than meat, so it remains a major part of the national diet. As a result, fishing is still important.

All over the world, bays and estuaries are used for fish farming. The fish are kept in underwater pens until they are large enough to sell.

Fish are farmed in these floating pens in a bay on the coast of Thailand in Southeast Asia.

Coastal defenses

The coast has been a barrier that island communities have fortified to keep out seaborne invaders. Along the southern coast of England, for example, a string of old castles is a reminder of the times when the British prepared to defend themselves against European enemies from across the narrow English Channel. More recent fortifications show that the British feared a German landing during World War II.

Trade and travel

Coasts became more important as trade expanded. During the sixteenth and seventeenth centuries, when explorers were opening up new lands, colonists settled along the coasts, using sheltered bays and estuaries as natural harbors where ships could load and unload in safety. Where natural harbors were not available, artificial ones were built and were protected from rough seas by high concrete walls.

Hong Kong has become an important city because it is situated on the coast.

Many of the world's major cities, such as New York, San Francisco, Hong Kong, Tokyo, and Sydney, owe their importance to their coastal locations. The trade from their harbors has brought these cities great wealth and power. Every year, vast amounts of freight are carried around the world by sea, so coasts continue to be important for international trade.

Huge ocean liners used to be a common sight in harbors. However, air travel has put most of these passenger lines out of business, and the majority of people who use harbors today are making short trips by ferry.

Power and industry
The development of ports has attracted industries to the coast,

Tidal power
This is a photograph of the dam that crosses the estuary of the Rance River in Brittany, northwest France. The 2,500-foot-long dam was completed in 1966. It was built to make use of the energy in tides. There are many tunnels through the dam. In each tunnel there is a turbine containing blades that are spun by water entering or leaving the estuary at high or low tide. The spinning turbines generate electricity for nearby homes. There are plans to build a similar dam across the estuary of the Severn River in England.

This power station, at Aberthaw in South Wales, has been built on the coast so that sea-water can be used to cool it.

since being near a port keeps transportation costs low. An added bonus is that often the land near a coast is low and flat—just what is needed for the construction of factories. Power stations for generating electricity are often located by the sea so that seawater can be used to cool the machinery. Now, scientists are developing ways of harnessing the power of waves and tides to generate electricity.

Some industrial uses of the coast
• *Sand and gravel are dredged up for use in the building industry.*
• *In hot countries, seawater is channeled into ponds. The sun evaporates the water, leaving the salt. In 1 pound of seawater there is 0.56 ounces of salt.*
• *Diamonds are mined on the seashore of Namibia, southern Africa.*
• *Oil and gas are often found offshore.*

Salt being removed from seawater on the coast of Sri Lanka, in the Indian Ocean

Health and leisure

The invention of steam and gasoline engines in the nineteenth century brought about great changes to many coasts. Previously, people rarely traveled far. Now it was possible for city dwellers to go to the shore and back again in a day. The vacation at the beach had been born. Easier travel also opened up the coast for all sorts of leisure activities, from land-based ones, such as rock climbing and walking, to water sports, such as sailing and scuba diving. Facilities had to be provided for all the day-trippers and vacationers. Hotels, restaurants, and amusement arcades were built to ensure that people enjoyed themselves. People returned relaxed and refreshed from the coast. They attributed this to the clean air, the slower pace of life away from the cities' hustle and bustle, and the milder climate. People went to the coast to recover from illnesses, and many older people moved there as a pleasant place to spend their retirement years.

The spread of low air fares has brought even greater changes to the coast. Trains, cars, and buses had given people the freedom to travel within their own country. Now, planes let them travel all over the world. Today, people fly for seaside vacations on the other side of the world. Huge coastal resorts, full of multistory hotels, have been constructed to cope with all the tourists arriving daily in jumbo jets. Tourism is a big and ever-increasing industry, and the coast is responsible for much of its growth.

Benidorm, in Spain, is one of the busiest seaside resorts in the world. People fly here for vacations from all over Europe.

A village in the Netherlands that was flooded during the storm of 1953. In many areas it was easier to travel by boat than by car.

Lives under threat

Many inland people think that people who live by the sea have a better life than they do, but that is not always true …

• *On the night of January 31, 1953, gale-force winds produced waves over 20 feet high in the North Sea. This storm coincided with spring tides and rivers full of winter rainwater emptying into the sea. As a result, the sea rose 8 feet higher than normal on England's southeastern coast and over 10 feet higher on the Dutch coast. In the Netherlands, 1,800 people were drowned, and in England, 264.*

• *The country of Bangladesh lies on the low land of the Ganges Delta in the Bay of Bengal in the Indian Ocean. Powerful tropical storms, called cyclones, push waves into the shallows at the top of the bay, where they turn into 26-foot-tall giants that thunder down onto Bangladesh's coast. In 1985, 40,000 Bangladeshis were killed when storms and giant waves hit the land.*

High mud embankments protect villages on the Ganges Delta from big waves during tropical storms.

8. PROTECTING THE COAST

As we have seen, coasts are under constant attack from the sea. Ever since people first settled by the sea, many coasts have been turned into battlegrounds where people have tried to keep the sea from harming their land.

Sea defenses

As their name implies, sea defenses are constructions for protecting the land from the sea's attack.

On many coasts, groins extend into the sea to stop longshore drift from removing beach material. They also reduce the power of breaking waves, so promenades and buildings on the seafront are not damaged. Groins are generally wooden fences, but some are now made of concrete.

A breakwater is a larger, concrete version of a groin. While groins are always straight, breakwaters can be curved. They are often built in front of harbors to shelter them from the worst of storms. Breakwaters also keep longshore drift from making harbors too shallow for ships.

Where the land is being severely eroded by the sea, concrete seawalls are put up to shield it from the waves.

Although sea defenses have been designed to benefit the coast, they also damage it. Because they act as barriers to longshore drift, groins and breakwaters can rob beaches of material. While material builds up on one part of the coast, it is stopped from reaching beaches farther along. As a result, these beaches may shrink, and the narrower they become the more waves can erode the land behind them. In solving one problem, sea defenses can create others. For this reason, many people argue against spending a lot of money on them. Instead, they suggest the money would be better

These groins keep the pebble beach from being removed by longshore drift.

These special "tetrapods" on the coast of Denmark lock together during storms to keep waves from hitting the land.

spent on moving people away from the coast. This may be possible in a large country, but in a small, coastal country such as the Netherlands, it is not. The Dutch have had no alternative but to defend themselves from the sea. Indeed, they have gone one step farther and taken back land overrun by it.

Fighting the sea Dutch style

The ancestors of present-day Dutch people settled on islands in the Rhine River Delta about 450 B.C. They were drawn there by the plentiful supply of fish. The delta land was marshy and low and easily flooded by the sea. To get around this problem, these first settlers built hillocks of earth, called *terpen,* where they would live when the water was high.

These windmills once pumped water out of marshy land in the Netherlands.

In the twelfth century, the delta people decided to build walls, or dikes, between the *terpen,* behind which villages could be built without fear of flooding.

Later in the Middle Ages, soldiers from the Crusades returned with a new idea for fighting the sea: windmills. If Arab farmers were using them to irrigate the land, perhaps the Dutch could use windmills to drain it. Soon the Rhine Delta's marshes were being enclosed by dikes and then drained by pumps powered by windmills—a simple but very effective solution. The land reclaimed from the sea was called a polder. Later, more powerful steam-driven pumps took over from the windmills. In the 1850s they were able to dry out more than 40,000 acres near Amsterdam.

Spurred on by this amazing achievement, Dutch engineers turned their attention to the Zuider Zee. This had been a small freshwater lake until, in the 1200s, waves had eaten away a gap of several miles in the coastline separating it from the North Sea. The sea had poured through the gap, turning the lake into an inland sea of more than 15,400 square miles and drowning hundreds of thousands of acres of precious farming land in the process. In the late 1800s, this land was needed to feed the Netherlands' growing population. Work on draining the Zuider Zee finally began in 1919, after years of debate about whether it was possible.

In 1932 a dam was completed across the gap in the coast. It contained locks to allow ships to pass through it and sluice gates. These were kept shut at high tide and opened at low tide to allow water to drain out of the Zuider Zee. Within five years it was a freshwater lake again; the seawater was pushed out by the Ijssel River that emptied into it. The Zuider Zee was renamed the

A drainage canal running through a reclaimed polder in the Netherlands. Once the saltwater has drained out of it, this land will be good for farming.

Ijsselmeer (Ijssel Sea) in its honor. Engineers then set to work to dry out the farmland covered by the lake. Thanks to the polders of the Ijsselmeer, the Netherlands has increased its land area by 5 percent. The Ijsselmeer has also provided the country with a large source of drinking water.

The severe storm in the winter of 1953 (*see* page 36) tore huge holes in the 400 miles of dikes along the Netherlands' southern coast, badly flooding the land and causing hundreds of deaths. Determined that this would never be repeated, the Dutch fought back. Copying their earlier work on the Zuider Zee, they built high dams across the Rhine River Delta, preventing the sea from flowing up the delta's channels. A network of smaller dams behind these high dams controlled the amount of water in the channels, ensuring that it never rose high enough to damage the dikes. Project Delta, as it was called, took 35 years to finish. Like the Zuider Zee before it, it has been a complete success.

Full of admiration for their achievements, a Frenchman once said: "God made the Earth, but the Dutch made Holland." As a result of the ingenuity of past and present engineers, the Dutch have pushed back the sea from their land. In doing so, they have been able to make use of the Rhine Delta's fertile, silty soil for agriculture. Today, protected by dikes, dams, and pumps, 40 percent of the Netherlands lies below sea level.

Many of the dams for Project Delta are wide enough for four lanes of traffic.

9. POLLUTING THE COAST

Our coasts are polluted in many ways: by farmers, industries, oil tankers, and the general public. Sometimes the pollution is caused by an accident, but more often than not, it is the result of a deliberate action.

Human waste

A major source of pollution is the untreated human waste, or sewage, from coastal towns and cities. Instead of being made harmless at water-

treatment plants, much human waste is allowed to flow directly into the sea. In Great Britain, for example, 300 million gallons of untreated sewage is pumped into the sea every day.

Besides being a health hazard to humans, the raw sewage affects wildlife along the shore. When the sewage decays, it uses up the oxygen in the water that plants and animals need for their survival.

The problem of sewage disposal is worst in developing countries, which have no money to build water-treatment plants. It is also a worry in many developed countries where much money needs to be spent on modernizing old treatment plants to keep up with expanding populations. In the European Union countries, a careful eye is kept on the quality of the water at popular beaches. "Blue flags" are awarded to the clean ones. Beaches that fail the test are required by law to be improved.

Less dangerous, but equally messy, is another form of human waste on the coast: the trash dropped by both local people and visitors. Aerosol cans, for example, can end up in rocky pools. If they are punctured, chemicals can leak out, which will harm the creatures living nearby. Sometimes, the litter found on the coast comes from abroad. Scientists say that 30 percent of all the litter on Scotland's beaches has been brought there by the Gulf Stream current from North America's east coast.

Above Sewage flows out onto a beach in the tourist resort of Rimini, Italy.

Right Trash left by tourists on a Caribbean island

Industrial waste

Many factories have been built on the coast so that their waste can be dumped into the sea. Toxic waste from factories can enter the coastal food chain and eventually end up harming humans. Between 1953 and 1960 over 100 people died and 2,000 were paralyzed after eating fish contaminated with mercury draining from a factory on the shores of Minamata Bay in Japan. Children were born blind or with deformed arms and legs as a consequence of their parents having eaten the poisoned seafood.

Many people are afraid that there will be an accident at a coastal nuclear power station that will let radioactive waste into the sea. There are already fears that the cooling water returned to the sea from these power stations is radioactive enough to make people ill.

Agricultural waste

Chemical fertilizers and pesticides used on farms drain into rivers and then into the sea. They contain nitrates and phosphates, which encourage the growth of algae. Algae forms a thick, green scum on top of the water, blocking out the sun from the seabed. The algae also removes oxygen from the water. Both these actions affect the development of other creatures and plants near the shore.

Poisonous waste

• *In January 1989 the* Sydney Morning Herald *newspaper published some disturbing statistics about the waste draining from one of the city's main sewage pipes. Some fish caught near it contained 122 times the safe level of a very poisonous chemical, benzene hexachloride.*

• *The Irish Sea off the west coast of Great Britain contains high levels of radioactive chemicals because cooling water from the Sellafield nuclear power station drains into it.*

• *Since the breakup of the USSR in 1991, unwanted nuclear weapons have been dumped off the coast of north Russia. Scientists are concerned that radioactive materials will leak out of them and spread into other oceans.*

Harmful algae floating in the sea off Sweden. The algae flourishes in the presence of agricultural chemicals that drain off fields into rivers.

Oil spills

A supertanker accident creates headline news and draws everyone's attention to the damage being done to the coast. It is estimated that nearly 4 million tons of oil spill into the sea every year. Most of this comes from tanker disasters, although a lot also comes from ships cleaning out their tanks at sea. The spilled oil oozes over many miles of coastline, coating the plants and animals living there. The oil mats the fluffy feathers of birds and the fur of mammals, such as otters, so they can no longer keep warm. Unless they are cleaned quickly, the animals die of cold. Clearing up the oil creates additional problems. Detergents have to be used that themselves can harm plants and animals.

A seabird killed by an oil spill in the North Sea

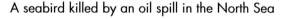

Oil Tanker Disasters

• *In 1967 the* Torrey Canyon *ran onto rocks off Land's End in southwest England: 118,000 tons of oil were spilled and 40,000 to 100,000 seabirds died.*

• *In 1978 the* Amoco Cadiz *went aground on the Brittany coast of northern France: 223,000 tons of oil gushed out, killing 48,000 seabirds and about 253,000 tons of fish and shellfish, including valuable lobsters and oysters. Some 186 miles of Brittany's coast was affected.*

• *In 1989 the* Exxon Valdez *hit rocks in Prince William Sound, Alaska, spilling 10 million gallons of oil. Within two weeks a 155-mile-long oil slick had damaged 4,200 sq. mi. of coastline. No other oil spill has killed so much wildlife, including 4,000 otters, 400,000 seabirds, 200 seals, and 13 killer whales.*

• *In 1993 the* Braer *ran aground on the Shetland Isles, Scotland: 100,000 tons of oil spilled out. Nearby salmon farms had to shut, and farmers' crops were ruined by oil blown inland.*

Clearing up oil in Alaska from the *Exxon Valdez* supertanker.

10. CARING FOR COASTS

In recent years people have become more aware of the need to care for their environments, including coasts. Many businesses have been reluctant to install expensive machinery to clean up their waste before it is dumped in the sea. Consequently, governments have had to pass laws making it compulsory for them to do so. Governments have also been trying to persuade shipping companies to use sea routes that keep their oil tankers as far away from land as possible, to reduce the chances of their running aground in bad weather or after engine failure. The British government is experimenting with spotter planes above the English Channel, which catch ships cleaning out their tanks. The ships' names are taken and their owners fined for creating an oil slick.

Governments, too, are trying to reduce the damage visitors cause to coastal areas. People not only leave trash, but also wear away the ground, uproot rare plants, and disturb nesting birds. In Great Britain, for example, Heritage Coastal Parks have been created. The parks have set routes for cyclists and walkers and noticeboards with conservation advice so that visitors can enjoy themselves while doing the least harm.

The problems of tourism
"The Indian resort of Goa is being destroyed by hotel owners trying to cash in on the growing tourist trade, claims Tourism Concern. Hotels are being blamed for illegally diverting scarce water supplies, says the group, discharging inadequately treated sewage into the sea and eradicating sand dunes to make way for lawns."
Geographical,
April 1995

A line of duckboards keeps visitors from wearing away these sand dunes, where there are many species of rare plants.

Similar parks are being set up all over the world—and not only on land. Because swimmers have been damaging the coral on Australia's Great Barrier Reef (*see* page 29), it has been turned into a marine park. People are allowed to visit only certain parts of it, and then a careful eye is kept on what they do. Other marine parks have been set up in Thailand and other countries, where restrictions are placed on the numbers of people visiting islands that have special or endangered species of plants or fish.

Coastal tourism earns a lot of money for many poor countries. It provides jobs for people who would otherwise have no work. However, it can upset the local balance of nature. In Belize, in Central America, building tourist resorts on the coast has involved draining mangrove swamps and filling them with soil from inland grasslands. Thus, two ecosystems have been ruined, which may create serious environmental problems in the future. Now, Belize is using satellites to map its mangrove swamps as part of a plan to develop the coast with the least possible harm to nature.

The coast is a precious place that needs protecting. Fortunately, governments all over the world are realizing this, and they are doing their best to ensure that it is not spoiled for future generations.

Scenes like this one in Oregon persuade people and governments to look after the coast.

Glossary

Aerosol cans   Containers filled with liquid under pressure from gas so that the liquid can be released as a fine spray.

Acidic   Sour; capable of burning the skin.

Algae   Seaweed and other similar plants.

Artificial   Made by humans rather than by nature.

Atmosphere   The layer of gases surrounding the earth.

Crustaceans   Creatures with a shell, such as lobsters, crabs, shrimps, and barnacles.

Current   A flow of water that moves steadily in one direction.

Dam   A barrier built to hold back flowing water.

Detergents   Chemicals used for cleaning. Detergents are used to clean up oil pollution.

Ecosystem   All plants and animals that live together in particular places.

Erosion   A wearing away of something.

Estuary   The wide lower part (or mouth) of a river through which it enters the sea.

Evaporate   To change into vapor as when a liquid is heated and turns into a gas.

Fauna   All the animals that live in a particular area.

Flora   All the plants in a particular area.

Glaciers   Rivers of ice.

Global warming   The term that describes the warming of the earth's climate because of the build up of "greenhouse gases."

Greenhouse gases   Gases, such as carbon dioxide, methane, and ozone, which keep heat from escaping through the atmosphere.

Habitat   The place where an animal or plant lives.

Headlands   Narrow areas of land jutting into the sea.

Hydraulic action   An action caused by the pressure of a liquid such as water.

Irrigation   Supplying the land with water by building canals and ditches.

Locks   Sections of a canal or river that can be closed by gates to control the water level.

Mercury   A heavy, silvery, poisonous liquid metallic element.

Mollusks   Soft animals without backbones and (usually) with hard shells, such as whelks, mussels, and oysters.

Nourishing   Feeding with something that is good and healthy for growth.

Nutritious   Having value as food.

Oil slick   A mass of oil floating on the surface of the water, usually after having leaked out of an oil tanker.

Plankton   Very tiny plants and animals floating in the sea.

Pollution   The spoiling of water, air, or land by harmful substances.

Predators   Animals that hunt other animals.

Radioactive   Giving off atomic rays, which are usually harmful.

Ria   A long, narrow inlet of the sea coast.

Satellites   Artificial objects that orbit the earth.

Silt   A mixture of particles of rocks and soil carried by a river.

Sluicegates   Gates used to control the flow of water in a channel.

Toxic   Highly poisonous.

Tributaries   Streams or rivers that flow into a larger river.

Turbine   An engine containing blades that are spun by the power of a moving fluid, such as water.

USSR   The former Union of Soviet Socialist Republics, a group of countries ruled by a communist government centered in Moscow. The USSR broke up in 1991.

BOOKS TO READ AND FURTHER INFORMATION

Books to Read:

Coote, Roger, ed. *Atlas of the Environment*. Milwaukee: Raintree Steck-Vaughn, 1992

Dixon, Dougal. *The Changing Earth*. Young Geographer. New York: Thomson Learning, 1993.

Fleisher, Paul. *Ecology A to Z*. New York: Dillon Press, 1994.

Hecht, Jeff. *Shifting Shores: Rising Seas, Retreating Shoreline*. New York: Scribners, 1990.

Javna, John. *Fifty Simple Things Kids Can Do to Save the Earth*. Kansas City, MO: Andrews & McMeel, 1990.

Kricher, John C. and Gordon Morrison. *Peterson's First Guide to Seashores*. Boston: Houghton Mifflin, 1992.

Parker, Steve. *Seashore* (Eyewitness Books). New York: Knopf, 1989.

Tesar, Jenny. *Endangered Habitats*. Our Fragile Planet. New York: Facts on File, 1992.

Useful Addresses:

For further information about habitats that may be under threat, contact the following environmental organizations:

Center for Environmental Education, Center for Marine Conservation, 1725 De Sales Street NW, Suite 500, Washington, DC 20036

Chesapeake Bay NERR-MD, Maryland Department of Natural Resources, Tawes Office Building, 580 Taylor Avenue, Annapolis, MD 21401

Fish and Wildlife Service, Department of the Interior, Washington, DC 20420

Friends of the Earth (U.S.A.), 218 D Street SE, Washington, DC 20003

Greenpeace U.S.A., 1436 U Street NW, Washington, DC 20009

National Audubon Society, National Education Office, R.R. #1, Box 171, Sharon, CT 06069

National Oceanic and Atmospheric Administration, Department of Commerce, Washington, DC 20230

World Wildlife Fund, 1250 24th Street NW, Washington, DC 20037

Picture acknowledgments

Bryan and Cherry Alexander Photography 19, 39 (lower). Associated Press/Topham 36 (top). Bruce Coleman/John Shaw *contents page*, 8, /Jan van de Kam 24 (top), /Steven C. Kaufman 24 (lower), /Jane Burton 25 (lower), /Allan G. Potts 27, /Andrew J. Purcell 30 (top), /Jeff Foott Productions 31 (top). David Cumming 10 (top), 20, 35, 37. Eye Ubiquitous/Paul Thompson *cover*, /Sportshoot 6, /Bruce Adams 11, /Pauline Thornton 13, /L. Fordyce 14, /David Batterbury 29 (top), /David Cumming 32 /Julia Waterlow 33 (top), /Kevin Wilton 34 (top). Geoscience Features 9, 10 (lower), 12, 15, 16, 21 (top), 22 (top), 37 (lower), 44. Natural History Photographic Agency/Stephen Krasemann 26, /Roy Waller 28. Popperfoto/Epoque Ltd 7. Still/Thierry Thomas 5 (lower), /Patrick Bertrand 21 (lower), /Andy Crump 22 (lower), /Brecelj and Hodalic 25, /Bruno Pambour 29 (lower), /Andre Fatras 30 (lower), /Julien Frebet 31, /Dominique Halleux 33, /Mark Edwards 34, 41 (top), /Julio Etchart/Reportage 41 (lower), /Andre Maslennikov 42, /Al Grillo 43. Tony Stone/Terry Donnelly *title page*, 45, /Xavier Lefaure 4, /Joe Cornish 5 (top), /H. Richard Johnston 7 (top), /Peter Cade 18, /David Woodfall 43 (top). Wayland Picture Library 36 (lower), 39 (top), 40.

Diagrams on pages 9, 11, 12, 15, 16, 17, and 23 by Peter Bull.

INDEX

Numbers in **bold** refer to photographs

DATE DUE
